A Practical Guide

1. Introduction

Introduction to Product Management

Definition and Importance of Product Management

Product Management is a complex and crucial discipline within any organization that develops products, whether software, hardware, services, or a combination of these. It represents the heartbeat of business innovation, guiding the entire product lifecycle from conception to realization, and ultimately to market withdrawal. But what exactly is Product Management, and why is it so important?

Definition of Product Management

Product Management can be defined as the collection of activities, skills, and processes

Successful Product Management

A Practical Guide

A. Luvaren

Copyright © 2024

that an organization implements to ideate, develop, launch, and improve a product. This process involves managing all phases of the product lifecycle, including market research, strategic planning, product development, market launch, user feedback management, and eventual product discontinuation.

Another way to describe Product Management is to consider it as the art and science of creating the right product for the right customer at the right time, and doing so in a sustainable and profitable way for the company. This definition highlights the essence of Product Management: the ability to balance customer needs and desires with the company's technical capabilities and resources, all within the context of dynamic and often competitive markets.

Importance of Product Management

The importance of Product Management cannot be overstated, especially in an increasingly complex and connected world where companies face global competition, rapid technological evolution, and rising consumer expectations. Here are some of the main reasons why Product Management is essential:

1. **Strategic Alignment**: Product Management ensures that the product is aligned with the company's vision, mission, and strategic goals. This alignment is crucial to ensure that the product not only meets customer needs but also contributes to the company's growth and sustainability in the long term.

2. **Market-Driven Innovation**: Effective Product Management is based on a deep understanding of the market and customer needs. This enables the company to develop innovative products that respond to emerging trends and changes in consumer preferences, staying ahead of the competition and establishing a competitive advantage.

3. **Risk Reduction**: Developing and launching a new product always involves risks, including market failure, excessive development costs, and unmet customer expectations. Product Management helps mitigate these risks through careful planning, requirement management, testing, and continuous feedback.

4. **Resource Optimization**: Corporate resources, such as time, money, and technical skills, are limited. Product Management ensures that these resources are used as efficiently as possible, focusing on the products and features that offer the most value.

5. **Product Lifecycle Management**: A product goes through various stages in its lifecycle, from conception to growth, maturity, and finally decline. Product Management is responsible for managing each of these stages, making informed decisions on when to launch a product, when to invest further in it, and when to eventually withdraw

it from the market.

6. **Customer-Centric Approach**: Product Management puts the customer at the center of every decision. This focus on customer satisfaction ensures that the products developed not only solve real customer problems but also create a positive experience that keeps them loyal to the company.

7. **Coordination Across Functions**: Product Management acts as a bridge between various corporate functions, including marketing, sales, development, operations, and customer support. This coordination role is essential to ensure that all parts of the organization work in synergy for the product's success.

In summary, Product Management is the engine that drives innovation and product success within a company. It is a discipline that requires a unique combination of analytical, strategic, and interpersonal skills, and has a direct impact on the company's ability to compete and thrive in an increasingly competitive global market.

Role of the Product Manager

The Product Manager is the professional who embodies the discipline of Product Management within an organization. Although the specific responsibilities of a Product Manager may vary depending on the company and industry, there are some key functions and skills that characterize this role.

Definition of the Product Manager's Role

A Product Manager is responsible for defining the strategy, roadmap, and features of a product or product line. This role requires a clear vision of the product, a deep understanding of the market and customers, and the ability to work effectively with multidisciplinary teams to bring the product from conception to commercialization.

The Product Manager is often described as the "mini-CEO" of the product. Although they do not necessarily have direct authority over all the corporate functions that contribute to the development and marketing of the product, they are responsible for the product's success or failure. This means that the Product Manager must be able to influence, negotiate, and guide teams through leadership and persuasion rather than hierarchical authority.

Skills and Attributes of a Product Manager

Becoming an effective Product Manager requires a combination of technical, analytical, and interpersonal skills, as well as a good dose of intuition and creativity. Here are some of the key skills a Product Manager must possess:

1. **Strategic Vision**: The Product Manager must be able to see the big picture and understand how the product fits into the overall corporate strategy. This requires a deep understanding of the market, competition, and emerging trends.

2. **Analytical Skills**: The ability to analyze complex data and draw meaningful conclusions is essential for the Product Manager. Whether analyzing product usage metrics, evaluating customer feedback, or comparing product performance with competitors, a data-driven approach is fundamental.

3. **Customer Empathy**: A good Product Manager must have a deep empathy for customers and an understanding of their needs, desires, and frustrations. This allows for the design of products that solve real problems and create value for users.

4. **Technical Competence**: While a

Product Manager does not necessarily need to be an engineer, it is important that they have an understanding of the technologies used to develop the product. This competence allows the Product Manager to communicate effectively with technical teams and make informed decisions about product features.

5. **Leadership and Communication**: The Product Manager must be able to lead cross-functional teams and communicate effectively with all stakeholders. This requires the ability to articulate a clear vision, negotiate compromises, and keep the team motivated and focused on the goals.

6. **Project Management**: Managing timelines, budgets, and resources is a crucial aspect of the Product Manager's job. This includes planning the product roadmap, managing risks, and ensuring that the product is delivered on time and within budget.

7. **Creativity and Innovation**: Finally, the

Product Manager must be able to think outside the box and propose innovative solutions to problems. This requires a creative mindset and a willingness to experiment and take calculated risks.

Key Responsibilities of the Product Manager

The responsibilities of a Product Manager can vary depending on the company size, industry, and the product's lifecycle stage. However, there are some common responsibilities that most Product Managers share:

1. **Market Research and Competitive Analysis**: The Product Manager is responsible for conducting market research to understand trends, market size, and consumer behavior. This also includes analyzing competitors to identify the product's strengths and weaknesses relative to the competition.

2. **Defining the Product Vision and Strategy**: One of the first and most important responsibilities of the Product Manager is to define the product vision and strategy. This involves setting clear goals, creating a product roadmap, and planning future features and releases.

3. **Managing the Backlog and Priorities**: The Product Manager is responsible for managing the product backlog, which is the list of features, changes, and improvements that need to be made to the product. This includes setting priorities based on customer value, market impact, and technical feasibility.

4. **Collaboration with Development Teams**: A significant portion of the Product Manager's work involves collaborating closely with development teams to ensure that the product is built according to the defined specifications and timelines. This includes participating in sprint meetings, reviewing technical specifications, and managing trade-offs.

5. **Product Launch and Go-to-Market Strategy**: The Product Manager works closely with marketing and sales teams to plan and coordinate the product launch. This includes defining the marketing message, planning advertising campaigns, and training the sales team.

6. **Collecting and Analyzing User Feedback**: After launch, the Product Manager is responsible for collecting and analyzing user feedback to identify areas for improvement and new development opportunities. This feedback is crucial for guiding future iterations of the product.

7. **Monitoring Product Performance**: The Product Manager monitors the product's performance through key metrics such as user adoption, customer satisfaction, and return on investment. These data are used to make informed decisions on how to evolve the product.

8. **Product Lifecycle Management**: Finally, the Product Manager is responsible for managing the product lifecycle, from market introduction to growth, maturity, and eventual decline. This includes critical decisions on when to update the product, when to retire it, and how to manage the transition to new products.

Challenges and Opportunities of the Product Manager Role

Being a Product Manager is a fascinating and challenging role, but also full of opportunities. Here are some of the main challenges and opportunities that Product Managers face:

1. **Managing Priorities and Trade-offs**: One of the most difficult challenges for a Product Manager is managing priorities and trade-offs. There are always more ideas and feature requests than can be implemented, and the Product Manager must be able to make tough decisions about what to develop and

what to delay.

2. **Communication and Alignment**: The Product Manager must communicate effectively with various stakeholders, each with their own priorities and goals. Keeping everyone aligned on the product vision and strategy can be challenging, especially in large or rapidly growing companies.

3. **Adapting to Change**: Markets and technologies change rapidly, and a Product Manager must be able to adapt and respond to these changes. This requires flexibility, agility, and the ability to learn and adapt continuously.

4. **Balancing Innovation and Practicality**: The Product Manager must balance the need to innovate with the practicality of what can be achieved with the available resources. This requires the ability to think creatively but also to be

grounded in reality.

5. **Opportunity for Impact**: Despite the challenges, the role of Product Manager offers an incredible opportunity to have a tangible impact on the success of the company. A successful product can drive company growth, open new markets, and significantly increase customer satisfaction.

In conclusion, the role of the Product Manager is complex and multifaceted, but it is also one of the most rewarding roles in an organization. For those who have the right combination of skills, determination, and passion, Product Management offers a unique opportunity to shape the future of products and drive business success.

The Product Development Process

The Product Development Process is the structured approach that organizations follow to conceive, design, develop, and bring a product to market. This process involves multiple stages, each with specific objectives, activities, and outcomes. A well-defined Product Development Process is essential for ensuring that the product meets customer needs, is technically feasible, and can be brought to market in a timely and cost-effective manner.

Phases of the Product Development Process

While the specific phases of the Product Development Process can vary depending on the industry and company, the following are the most common stages:

1. **Ideation and Concept Development**: The first phase of the process is ideation, where ideas for new products are generated. This can come from various sources, including customer feedback, market research, competitor analysis, and internal

brainstorming sessions. Once a viable idea is identified, a concept is developed that outlines the product's value proposition, target market, key features, and potential benefits.

2. **Feasibility Analysis and Business Case Development**: Before moving forward with product development, it is crucial to assess the feasibility of the concept. This involves evaluating technical feasibility, market potential, and financial viability. A business case is then developed that outlines the expected costs, revenue, and return on investment (ROI) of the product.

3. **Design and Prototyping**: In this phase, the product concept is translated into a detailed design. This includes creating prototypes that can be tested and refined. Prototyping allows the development team to experiment with different designs, identify potential issues, and gather feedback from users before committing to full-scale production.

4. **Development and Testing**: Once the design is finalized, the development phase begins. This involves building the product, whether it is a physical product, software application, or service. Throughout development, rigorous testing is conducted to ensure that the product meets quality standards, is free of defects, and performs as expected.

5. **Market Preparation and Launch**: As the product nears completion, preparations for the market launch begin. This includes developing a go-to-market strategy, which covers pricing, positioning, distribution channels, and marketing campaigns. The launch phase culminates with the introduction of the product to the market, where it is made available to customers.

6. **Post-Launch Evaluation and Iteration**: After the product is launched, it is essential to monitor its performance and gather customer feedback. This information is used to make necessary adjustments and improvements to

the product. The post-launch phase also includes evaluating the product's success against the original business case and making decisions on future iterations or updates.

Importance of Each Phase

Each phase of the Product Development Process plays a critical role in ensuring the success of the product. Skipping or rushing through any phase can lead to significant risks, including poor product quality, missed market opportunities, and financial losses. Here is why each phase is important:

1. **Ideation and Concept Development**: This phase is crucial for identifying opportunities and ensuring that the product concept aligns with market needs and company goals. It sets the foundation for the entire development process.

2. **Feasibility Analysis and Business Case

Development**: Conducting a thorough feasibility analysis helps prevent costly mistakes by ensuring that the product is technically achievable and financially viable. The business case provides a clear rationale for investing in the product.

3. **Design and Prototyping**: The design and prototyping phase is essential for translating the product concept into a tangible form. Prototyping allows for early detection of design flaws and provides an opportunity to gather user feedback before full-scale production.

4. **Development and Testing**: This phase ensures that the product is built to the required specifications and meets quality standards. Testing is critical for identifying and resolving issues that could impact the product's performance and customer satisfaction.

5. **Market Preparation and Launch**: The success of the product launch depends on

careful planning and execution. A well-crafted go-to-market strategy helps ensure that the product reaches the right customers, at the right time, and with the right message.

6. **Post-Launch Evaluation and Iteration**: Continuous improvement is key to maintaining a product's relevance and competitiveness in the market. The post-launch phase provides valuable insights that inform future product development and updates.

In conclusion, the Product Development Process is a structured approach that guides the creation of a product from concept to market. By following this process, companies can increase the likelihood of developing successful products that meet customer needs, deliver value, and drive business growth.

2. The Product Life Cycle (Product Life Cycle)

The product life cycle is a fundamental concept in Product Management and marketing. It describes the different stages a product goes through, from its conception to its withdrawal from the market. Understanding this cycle is essential for Product Managers, as it allows them to plan appropriate strategies for each stage, maximizing the product's value and ensuring long-term success.

Stages of the Product Life Cycle

The product life cycle is typically divided into four main stages: introduction, growth, maturity, and decline. Each stage has unique characteristics, challenges, and opportunities, and requires a specific strategic approach.

1. Introduction Stage

Characteristics of the Introduction Stage

The introduction stage is the starting point of the product life cycle. At this stage, the product is launched into the market for the first time. Often, the product is still in an early development phase, with limited features and a relatively small user base. The main objectives of this stage are to create product awareness, attract early customers, and start building a market base.

Challenges of the Introduction Stage

- **Low Brand Awareness**: During the introduction, the product is often unknown to most potential customers, making it difficult to attract attention.

- **High Costs**: Launching a new product can involve high costs, including research and development, marketing, and distribution.

- **High Risk**: Not all launched products

succeed in capturing market interest. There is always a risk that the product may not achieve the expected success.

Strategies for the Introduction Stage

1. **Aggressive Marketing**: To overcome low brand awareness, it's essential to implement aggressive marketing campaigns. These can include targeted advertising, special promotions, and launch events. The goal is to generate interest and curiosity around the new product.

2. **Strategic Pricing**: There are two main approaches to pricing during the introduction stage: market penetration and skimming. Market penetration involves setting a low price to quickly attract a large customer base, while skimming involves setting a high initial price to maximize profits from early adopters willing to pay more.

3. **Focus on Quality and Innovation**: To stand out from competitors, the product must offer unique value. This can be achieved through innovative features, superior design, or exceptional customer service.

4. **Development of Distribution Network**: It's important to establish effective distribution channels that make the product easily accessible to consumers. This can include forming partnerships with retailers, distributors, or online platforms.

2. Growth Stage

Characteristics of the Growth Stage

If the product successfully passes the introduction stage, it enters the growth stage. At this point, demand for the product begins to increase rapidly, the customer base expands, and revenues grow significantly. The product may start benefiting from economies of scale, and profit margins can improve.

Challenges of the Growth Stage

- **Increasing Competition**: As demand grows, new competitors are likely to enter the market, seeking to capture market share.

- **Production Management**: With increasing sales, it's necessary to ensure that production capacity is sufficient to meet demand without compromising quality.

- **Need for Continuous Innovation**: As the market expands, it's important to continue innovating to keep the product attractive and relevant.

Strategies for the Growth Stage

1. **Product Line Expansion**: During the growth stage, it may be useful to expand the product line to include variants, accessories, or premium versions. This helps capture a

larger market share and meet a broader range of customer needs.

2. **Strengthening Brand Identity**: Building a strong brand identity is crucial at this stage. This includes increasing brand visibility through targeted advertising campaigns and enhancing the product's reputation through positive reviews and customer testimonials.

3. **Distribution Optimization**: To reach a wider audience, it may be necessary to expand distribution channels. This could include entering new geographic markets or using new sales platforms, such as e-commerce.

4. **Dynamic Pricing**: During the growth stage, adopting a dynamic pricing strategy to maximize profits can be beneficial. This could include offering volume discounts, promotional packages, or special deals for loyal customers.

3. Maturity Stage

Characteristics of the Maturity Stage

The maturity stage is characterized by a slowdown in sales growth, as the product reaches peak market penetration. Most potential customers have already purchased the product, and competition is often intense. At this stage, the market is saturated, and differentiation becomes more difficult.

Challenges of the Maturity Stage

- **Intense Competition**: With the market nearing saturation, competitors seek to gain market share primarily through price and service.

- **Erosion of Profit Margins**: As price-based competition increases, profit margins may begin to shrink.

- **Product Fatigue**: Customers may

become less enthusiastic about the product, which can lead to a decline in sales.

Strategies for the Maturity Stage

1. **Product Differentiation and Updates**: To maintain customer interest, it's important to introduce regular product updates. This could include new features, performance improvements, or a design overhaul.

2. **Market Position Consolidation**: During the maturity stage, it may be helpful to focus on consolidating your market position rather than expanding. This could include improving customer service, offering loyalty programs, or introducing post-sales services.

3. **Cost Optimization**: With increasing pressure on profit margins, it's essential to optimize production, distribution, and marketing costs. This might include automating processes, negotiating better terms

with suppliers, or reducing waste.

4. **Expansion into New Markets**: If the current market is saturated, it may be useful to explore new geographic markets or customer segments. This could include internationalizing the product or adapting it to meet the needs of a new customer group.

4. Decline Stage

Characteristics of the Decline Stage

The decline stage occurs when the product starts to lose relevance in the market. Sales decrease, profit margins further reduce, and the product may become obsolete due to new technologies or changes in consumer preferences. At this stage, companies must decide whether to maintain the product, improve it, or withdraw it from the market.

Challenges of the Decline Stage

- **Declining Sales**: With declining sales, it can become difficult to justify further investment in the product.

- **Technological Obsolescence**: New technologies or more advanced competing products can render the product obsolete.

- **Changing Consumer Preferences**: Consumers may shift their focus to newer and more innovative products, leaving the current product at a disadvantage.

Strategies for the Decline Stage

1. **Gradual Product Withdrawal**: One of the most common strategies during the decline stage is the gradual withdrawal of the product from the market. This includes reducing inventory, cutting production, and discontinuing product promotion.

2. **Cost Reduction**: To maintain profitability during the decline, it's essential to reduce the costs associated with the product. This might include closing dedicated production lines, reducing involved staff, or discontinuing less profitable distribution channels.

3. **Development of Budget Versions**: In some cases, it may be useful to develop budget or simplified versions of the product to exploit low-cost markets or attract more price-sensitive consumers.

4. **Sale or Licensing of the Product**: If the product still has residual value, it might be appropriate to sell it or license the technology or brand to another company that could better exploit the remaining niche market.

General Strategies for the Product Life Cycle

In addition to specific strategies for each stage, there are general approaches that Product Managers can adopt to effectively manage the product life cycle.

1. Continuous Innovation

Continuous innovation is one of the most important strategies for keeping a product competitive throughout all stages of its life cycle. This includes not only the introduction of new features but also constant updates to the technologies used, adaptation to emerging market trends, and improvements in the user experience.

2. Data Analysis and Adaptation

Using data to guide product decisions is crucial for long-term success. Product Managers must constantly monitor key metrics, such as sales, customer satisfaction, reviews, and user behavior. This data can provide valuable insights on how to adapt the product and marketing strategies in response to market changes.

3. Flexibility and Adaptability

In a dynamic market, the ability to quickly adapt to changes is crucial. This means being ready to modify product strategies, rapidly introduce new features, or change direction when necessary. Product Managers must be flexible and prepared to make quick decisions to capitalize on new opportunities or mitigate unforeseen risks.

4. Product Portfolio Management

In companies with multiple products, it is important to manage the product portfolio strategically. This includes evaluating the life cycle of each product, identifying synergies between products, and deciding which products to promote, update, or withdraw.

Effective portfolio management helps maximize overall profits and avoid sales cannibalization between similar products.

The product life cycle is an essential concept for understanding how products develop and evolve over time. Each stage of the life cycle presents unique challenges and opportunities, and requires specific strategies to maximize product success. Product Managers play a crucial role in this process, guiding the product through its various stages, from introduction to decline, and adopting innovative and adaptable approaches to ensure that the product remains competitive and profitable over time. With careful and strategic management, it is possible to extend the product's life cycle, maximizing return on investment and contributing to the company's long-term success.

3. Market Research

Market research is a crucial activity for any business that seeks to better understand its industry, consumer behavior, and competitive dynamics. For a Product Manager, market research is not just a preliminary phase in product development but an ongoing process that supports informed decision-making throughout the entire product lifecycle. Through market research, companies can gather valuable data, analyze competitors, and identify the target audience, ensuring that the product meets market needs and is competitively positioned.

Data Collection Methods

Data collection is the first fundamental step in market research. The data gathered forms the basis for subsequent analyses and helps inform strategic decisions. Various data collection methods exist, each with its own advantages and disadvantages. Product

Managers must choose the most appropriate method or combination of methods based on the specific objectives of the research and the resources available.

1. Primary Data Collection

Primary data collection involves the direct gathering of new information specifically for the purposes of the current research. This type of data is customized and can provide detailed and specific insights into a problem or research question.

Primary Data Collection Methods

- **Surveys**: Surveys are one of the most common methods for collecting primary data. They can be conducted online, by phone, by mail, or in person. Surveys allow the collection of information on a wide range of topics, such as consumer preferences, purchasing habits, and brand perception.

Survey design is crucial; questions must be clear, concise, and unbiased to obtain reliable data.

- **Interviews**: Interviews, whether structured or unstructured, allow for an in-depth exploration of participants' opinions and experiences. Interviews can be conducted face-to-face, by phone, or via video calls. This method provides an opportunity to explore respondents' answers in more detail and obtain qualitative insights that may not emerge from a simple survey.

- **Focus Groups**: Focus groups involve guided discussions with a small group of participants representing the target audience. These meetings offer a dynamic environment where participants can share their opinions, ideas, and reactions to a product or concept. Focus groups are useful for exploring attitudes, perceptions, and motivations more deeply than surveys.

- **Observation**: Direct observation of consumer behavior in their natural environment, such as in a store or during product use, can provide valuable data that does not emerge through self-reporting methods like surveys and interviews. Observation can be conducted openly, where participants are aware of being observed, or covertly, to minimize influence on their behavior.

- **Experiments**: Experiments are a primary research method that allows testing the effectiveness of specific variables, such as price or packaging, in a controlled environment. Experiments can be conducted in a lab or in the field and are useful for determining cause-and-effect relationships between variables.

2. Secondary Data Collection

Secondary data consists of information that has already been collected and is available from other sources. This data can come from published reports, industry studies, government statistics, newspaper articles, and other sources. Secondary data collection is often less expensive and faster than primary data collection, but it may be less relevant or detailed for the specific needs of the research.

Sources of Secondary Data

- **Academic Publications and Industry Studies**: Research conducted by academic institutions and industry organizations often provides detailed and in-depth analyses of specific topics, such as market trends, consumer behavior, and competitive dynamics.

- **Market Research Reports**: Numerous consulting and research firms publish market reports that provide data and analysis on various sectors. These reports are a valuable resource for understanding market size, competitors' market shares, and emerging trends.

- **Government Statistics**: Government agencies, such as ISTAT in Italy or the Census Bureau in the United States, regularly publish statistical data that can be used to analyze demographic, economic, and consumer trends.

- **Company Internal Data**: Companies often possess a vast amount of internal data, such as historical sales, customer behavior analyses, and feedback received from support channels. This data can be used to analyze product performance and identify areas for improvement.

3. Online Data Collection Techniques

With the advent of digital technologies, online data collection has become an essential part of market research. These methods offer an efficient way to reach a broad and diverse audience and collect data in real time.

Online Data Collection Methods

- **Online Surveys**: Online surveys are a quick and convenient way to collect data from a large audience. They can be distributed via email, social media, or embedded in websites. Online surveys can be easily customized and automated to collect responses on various topics.

- **Social Media Listening**: Social media listening involves monitoring online conversations on social networks to gather information on how consumers perceive a brand, product, or service. This method provides both qualitative and quantitative data that can be used to better understand market opinions and trends.

- **Web Analytics Data Analysis**: Analyzing data collected through web analytics tools, such as Google Analytics, can provide valuable insights into user behavior online. This data can include metrics such as website traffic, conversion rates, time spent on the site, and most visited pages, which can be used to optimize marketing strategies and product design.

- **Crowdsourcing**: Crowdsourcing is a technique where a company engages a large number of people to gather ideas, solutions, or data. This method is useful for generating a large amount of data quickly and often at low costs. Platforms like Amazon Mechanical Turk and other crowdsourcing networks are examples of how companies can use this method to collect data.

Competitor Analysis

Competitor analysis is a critical component of market research. It allows companies to better understand the competitive landscape and develop strategies that position them favorably in the market. For a Product Manager, competitor analysis is essential to identify strengths and weaknesses, opportunities and threats, and to define a product strategy that differentiates the company's offering.

1. Identifying Competitors

The first step in competitor analysis is to identify who the main competitors are. This process includes not only direct competitors (i.e., those offering similar products in the same market) but also indirect competitors who may meet the same customer needs with different solutions.

Types of Competitors

- **Direct Competitors**: These are competitors offering very similar products or services and competing for the same customer base. For example, Coca-Cola and Pepsi are direct competitors in the soft drink market.

- **Indirect Competitors**: These are competitors that offer different products that may satisfy the same customer needs. For example, for a restaurant, an indirect competitor might be a meal delivery service.

- **Potential Competitors**: These are companies that are not currently operating in the same market but could enter in the future, representing a potential threat. These competitors may come from other sectors or foreign markets.

2. Gathering Information on Competitors

Once competitors are identified, it is essential to gather detailed information about them. This can include data on their product offerings, pricing, marketing strategies, distribution, and market positioning.

Sources of Information on Competitors

- **Competitors' Websites**: Corporate websites provide a significant amount of information, including product details, prices, marketing strategies, and company communications. Regularly monitoring competitors' websites is a standard practice in competitive analysis.

- **Market Research Reports**: Many agencies publish reports that include detailed analyses of market shares, competitors' strategies, and industry trends. These reports are useful for gaining an overview of competitive dynamics.

- **Advertising and Marketing**: Analyzing competitors' advertising campaigns and marketing strategies can offer insights into their positioning strategies and efforts to reach the target audience.

- **Customer Interviews and Feedback**: Talking directly with customers who have purchased competitors' products can provide valuable information on perceived strengths and weaknesses, as well as customer satisfaction levels. Feedback on social media and online reviews are other important sources of information.

- **Financial Analysis**: If competitors are public companies, their financial reports are publicly available. These documents provide insights into financial performance, R&D investments, marketing expenditures, and growth strategies.

- **Networking and Industry Events**: Attending trade shows, conferences, and other industry events can provide an opportunity to gather direct information on competitors and their new initiatives.

3. Evaluating Competitors' Strategies

After gathering all the necessary information,

the next step is to evaluate competitors' strategies. This process involves analyzing their strengths and weaknesses, opportunities and threats (SWOT analysis), as well as their competitive position in the market.

Key Elements to Analyze

- **Value Proposition**: What is the unique value proposition of the competitors? What do they offer that sets them apart from others? Understanding this helps define your own value proposition so that it resonates better with the target audience.

- **Market Positioning**: How do competitors position themselves in the market in terms of price, quality, and customer target? Identifying competitors' positioning helps understand how they differentiate themselves and where there are opportunities to position more effectively.

- **Pricing Strategies**: Competitors' pricing strategies are a critical factor. Some may compete on low prices, while others may aim for premium pricing to position themselves as quality leaders. Understanding these strategies helps determine your own pricing policy.

- **Distribution Strategies**: Analyzing how competitors distribute their products is essential. Some may focus on a strong online presence, while others may have a well-developed physical distribution network. Knowing these strategies helps optimize your distribution channels.

- **Innovation and R&D**: Innovation is often a key driver of competitiveness. Examining competitors' investments in research and development can reveal their ability to innovate and launch new products in the market.

- **Differentiating Factors**: What are the factors that distinguish one competitor from the others? It could be the technology used, design, sustainability, customer service, or other aspects that create a competitive advantage.

4. Strategic Planning Based on Competitor Analysis

After completing competitor analysis, the Product Manager can use the gathered information to inform product strategic planning. This can include modifying the product strategy, optimizing the value proposition, adjusting pricing, or identifying new market opportunities.

Steps in Strategic Planning

- **Defining the Value Proposition**:

 Based on the analysis of competitors' strengths and weaknesses, define a unique value proposition that clearly differentiates your product from others on the market.

- **Target Market Selection**: Identify which market segments are less served by competitors and tailor your offering to meet the specific needs of these segments.

- **Product Positioning**: Develop a clear and distinctive positioning strategy that resonates with the target audience. This may involve emphasizing aspects such as quality, innovation, or customer experience.

- **Pricing Strategy**: Based on competitors' pricing strategies and your own value proposition, develop a pricing strategy that is competitive while ensuring profitability.

- **Distribution Channels**: Analyze the effectiveness of competitors' distribution channels and identify new opportunities or partnerships to improve your own distribution strategy.

- **Innovation Strategy**: Plan R&D investments based on the analysis of competitors' innovation capabilities, ensuring the continuous development of new products and technologies.

5. Continual Monitoring and Adjustment

Competitor analysis is not a one-time task but requires continuous monitoring and adjustments. The competitive landscape is constantly evolving, with new competitors entering the market and existing ones changing their strategies. Regularly updating competitor analysis ensures that the company's product strategies remain relevant and competitive.

Importance of Continuous Monitoring

- **Early Identification of Threats and Opportunities**: By continuously monitoring competitors, a company can quickly identify emerging threats, such as a new competitor or changes in customer preferences. At the same time, it can identify new opportunities, such as a market gap or a competitor's weakness.

- **Adapting to Market Changes**: The market environment is dynamic, and companies need to be agile to respond to changes. Continuous monitoring of competitors enables timely adjustments to product strategy, pricing, and distribution.

- **Sustaining Competitive Advantage**: Maintaining a competitive advantage requires ongoing effort. Competitor analysis helps ensure that the company remains competitive by continuously improving its product offering and customer experience.

Tools for Ongoing Monitoring

- **Competitive Intelligence Software**: There are various software tools available that allow for automated monitoring of competitors, including tracking changes on their websites, analyzing their marketing campaigns, and monitoring customer reviews.

- **Google Alerts and Social Media Monitoring**: Setting up Google Alerts and using social media monitoring tools can help track mentions of competitors and gather information in real-time about their activities.

- **Regular Market Research Updates**: Regularly updating market research reports ensures that the company remains informed of the latest trends and changes in the competitive landscape.

In conclusion, market research and competitor analysis are essential components of the Product Manager's role. By systematically collecting and analyzing data on the market and competitors, Product Managers can make informed decisions that lead to the development of products that meet market needs, are competitively positioned, and ultimately drive business success. The continuous nature of this process ensures that companies remain agile, proactive, and capable of sustaining their competitive advantage in a rapidly evolving marketplace.

4. Product Development

Product development is a complex process that spans from the initial idea to its realization and market launch. Each phase of this process is critical and requires a combination of creativity, strategy, and cross-functional collaboration to ensure the final product meets customer needs and market expectations. In this discussion, we will explore three key phases of product development: ideation and brainstorming, prototyping and testing, and collaboration with the development team.

Ideation and Brainstorming

Ideation is the initial phase of the product development process, where ideas for new products or improvements to existing ones are generated. This phase is crucial as it lays the foundation for all subsequent work. During ideation, teams aim to identify problems to solve, market opportunities to capitalize on, and innovative concepts that could bring value to both the company and customers.

1. Ideation Process

The ideation process often begins with understanding market and customer needs. This requires thorough market research, which may include analyzing trends, listening to customers, studying competitors, and evaluating new technologies.

Phases of the Ideation Process

- **Research and Analysis**: In this phase, teams gather relevant information on market trends, consumer behavior, emerging technologies, and competition. This research provides the necessary context for ideation and helps identify the most promising opportunities.

- **Problem Identification**: The next step is to identify problems or unmet needs in the market that could be addressed with a new product. This can include problems expressed directly by customers or discovered through observation and data analysis.

- **Idea Generation**: With a clear understanding of the problems and opportunities, teams can begin generating ideas for new products. This phase may involve various brainstorming techniques, which will be discussed later.

- **Idea Evaluation**: Not all generated ideas will be feasible or beneficial. The evaluation phase involves selecting the most promising ideas based on criteria such as technical feasibility, market potential, development costs, and alignment with company strategy.

- **Concept Development**: The selected ideas are then turned into more detailed product concepts. This may include defining key features, initial design, and the product's unique value proposition.

2. Brainstorming Techniques

Brainstorming is a technique used to generate a large number of ideas in a short period. It is a collaborative process that involves team members contributing ideas and suggestions. The success of brainstorming depends on an open and non-judgmental environment where all ideas are considered valid, and none are dismissed too quickly.

Common Brainstorming Techniques

- **Brainwriting**: Instead of discussing ideas aloud, participants write their ideas on paper or type them on computers. This method helps overcome barriers related to shyness or dominant thinking by some group members.

- **Mind Mapping**: Mind maps are a visual tool that helps explore ideas related to a central concept. It starts with a central word or idea in the middle of a page and then expands with branches representing related ideas, each with its own subcategories.

- **Six Thinking Hats**: This technique, developed by Edward de Bono, requires participants to look at the problem from six different perspectives (or "hats"). These include facts, emotions, negativity, positivity, creativity, and management. Each "hat" helps explore the problem more thoroughly and systematically.

- **SCAMPER**: SCAMPER stands for Substitute, Combine, Adapt, Modify, Put to another use, Eliminate, and Rearrange. This technique pushes participants to examine the current idea through these seven filters, leading to the generation of new ideas or variations.

- **Reverse Brainstorming**: Instead of asking how to solve a problem, participants are asked to think of ways to worsen the situation. Once these ideas are generated, the team works backward to find solutions that address the highlighted problems.

3. Idea Evaluation

After brainstorming, it is necessary to evaluate the generated ideas to select those with the greatest potential. This selection process requires clear and objective criteria and a deep understanding of the company's resources and capabilities.

Idea Evaluation Criteria

- **Technical Feasibility**: Is the idea technically feasible? Does the company have the skills and resources needed to develop the product?

- **Market Appeal**: Is there a market for the product? Is the potential demand sufficient to justify the investment?

- **Strategic Alignment**: Does the idea align with the company's vision, mission, and strategic objectives?

- **Profitability**: What are the potential revenues and profits? Can the development and production costs be covered by the expected sales?

- **Sustainability**: Can the product be developed and launched sustainably? What does it mean for the environment and society?

- **Differentiation**: Is the idea sufficiently unique to stand out from competing products? Does it offer value that customers cannot get elsewhere?

Once ideas are evaluated, the selected ones are further developed, often through the creation of a business case and approval from corporate management. From here, the project moves to the next phase of the development cycle: prototyping and testing.

Prototyping and Testing

The prototyping and testing phase is crucial for transforming a conceptual idea into a tangible product. This phase allows the development team to build preliminary versions of the product, test them, and refine the design and functionality before proceeding to large-scale production. Through prototyping and testing, companies can reduce the risks associated with product launch, ensuring that it meets customer expectations and technical and market requirements.

1. Prototyping

Prototyping is the process of creating preliminary models of a product. These prototypes can range from simple physical or digital representations to fully functional versions of the product. The level of detail and functionality of the prototype depends on the specific purpose of the prototyping at that stage of development.

Types of Prototypes

- **Low-Fidelity Prototypes**: These prototypes are often used in the early stages of development to explore design concepts and ideas. They can include paper sketches, digital wireframes, or cardboard models. Low-fidelity prototypes are inexpensive and easy to modify, making them ideal for rapid experimentation.

- **High-Fidelity Prototypes**: These are more advanced models that closely resemble the final product in terms of appearance, function, and materials. High-fidelity prototypes are often used to test the product's functionality, usability, and aesthetic design.

- **Functional Prototypes**: These prototypes are fully functional versions of the product used to test mechanics, electronics, software, and other technical features. While they may not have the final product's appearance, they faithfully replicate its main functions.

- **Digital Prototypes**: In the case of software or technology-based products, digital prototypes are used to simulate the user interface, workflow, and functionalities. Tools like Figma, Adobe XD, and Sketch are commonly used to create interactive prototypes of applications and websites.

- **Rapid Prototypes**: This term refers to the quick construction of prototypes using technologies such as 3D printing, laser cutting, and CNC milling. Rapid prototyping allows teams to quickly iterate on design, testing, and improving the product in short cycles.

2. Testing Methodologies

Once prototypes are created, the next phase involves testing them to ensure that the product functions as expected and meets customer requirements. Testing is essential to identify defects, improve performance, and ensure that the product is market-ready.

Types of Tests

- **Usability Testing**: These tests assess how easy and intuitive the product is to use. They involve real users interacting with the prototype while the team observes and collects feedback. Usability testing helps identify issues with the user interface, workflow, and other features that can affect the user experience.

- **Performance Testing**: These tests measure the product's capabilities in terms of speed, endurance, durability, and other performance metrics. They are particularly important for products that must operate under extreme conditions or sustain heavy loads.

- **Reliability Testing**: These tests verify the product's ability to function correctly over an extended period without failures. They include endurance tests, life cycle tests, and stress tests to ensure the product is robust and reliable over time.

- **Compliance Testing**: These tests ensure that the product meets all relevant industry regulations and standards. They may include verifying compliance with safety, environmental, electrical, and quality regulations.

- **A/B Testing**: In software development, A/B testing is commonly used to compare two versions of a product or feature. Users are divided into groups, and each group tests a different version. This method helps determine which version of the product performs better in terms of engagement, conversions, or other key metrics.

- **System Integrity Testing**: These tests verify how the product works in combination with other systems and components. For example, a new hardware component might be tested to ensure it functions correctly with existing software and vice versa.

3. Iteration and Improvement

After running the tests, it is essential to collect and analyze the results to make necessary modifications to the prototype. This continuous iteration process is critical to refining the product and ensuring it meets all expectations before launch.

Iteration Process

- **Feedback Collection**: After each testing cycle, user feedback and performance data are collected and analyzed. This feedback can come from end users, internal testers, corporate stakeholders, and other relevant sources.

- **Data Analysis**: The team analyzes the collected data to identify recurring problems, areas for improvement, and opportunities to optimize the product. Analysis tools may include statistical analysis software, qualitative surveys, and technical reviews.

- **Modifications and Improvements**: Based on the analysis results, the team makes changes to the product's design, code, or mechanics. These improvements are implemented in the next prototype, which is then subjected to further testing.

- **Multiple Iterations**: This cycle of testing and improvement may be repeated many times until the product reaches the desired level of quality and performance. Each iteration brings the product one step closer to its final form.

- **Final Evaluation**: Once iterations are completed, the final prototype is evaluated to ensure it is ready for large-scale production or launch. This final evaluation includes a comprehensive review

of all test data, risk assessments, and compliance with industry standards.

Collaboration with the Development Team

Effective collaboration between different departments and disciplines is essential for the success of the product development process. From ideation to prototyping and testing, close communication and collaboration among team members ensure that each aspect of the product is developed coherently and efficiently.

1. Cross-Functional Teams

A cross-functional team brings together members from various departments, such as design, engineering, marketing, and sales. These teams leverage the diverse expertise of their members to develop a well-rounded product that meets technical, market, and user requirements.

Key Roles in a Cross-Functional Team

- **Product Manager**: The product manager oversees the entire development process, ensuring the product meets business goals, market needs, and user requirements. They coordinate between different departments and stakeholders, managing timelines, budgets, and resources.

- **Designers**: Designers are responsible for the product's aesthetics, usability, and user experience. They work closely with engineers and marketers to ensure the product looks appealing and is easy to use.

- **Engineers**: Engineers handle the technical aspects of product development, including the mechanics, electronics, and software. They ensure the product is functional, reliable, and scalable.

- **Marketers**: Marketers focus on the product's positioning, branding, and market launch. They conduct market research, define the target audience, and develop marketing strategies to promote the product.

- **Sales Representatives**: Sales representatives provide insights into customer needs and preferences. They work with the development team to ensure the product meets customer expectations and is attractive to the target market.

- **Quality Assurance (QA)**: QA professionals are responsible for testing the product to ensure it meets quality standards.

They work closely with engineers to identify and fix issues before the product is released.

- **Supply Chain and Operations**: These team members ensure the product can be produced, distributed, and delivered efficiently. They manage logistics, sourcing, manufacturing, and other operational aspects.

2. Communication Tools and Strategies

Effective communication is the cornerstone of successful collaboration in product development. Teams must be able to share information, provide feedback, and make decisions quickly and efficiently.

Communication Tools

- **Project Management Software**: Tools like Trello, Asana, Jira, and Monday.com help teams manage tasks, track progress, and collaborate on projects. These platforms provide a central hub for team communication and project management.

- **Communication Platforms**: Platforms like Slack, Microsoft Teams, and Zoom facilitate real-time communication and collaboration. Teams can use these tools for meetings, chats, video calls, and document sharing.

- **Collaboration Software**: Tools like Google Drive, Notion, and Miro allow teams to collaborate on documents, designs, and projects in real time. These platforms enable seamless sharing and editing of files and ideas.

Communication Strategies

- **Regular Check-ins**: Regular meetings and updates are essential to keep the team aligned on progress, issues, and next steps. Daily stand-ups, weekly reviews, and milestone meetings are common practices.

- **Open Feedback Culture**: An open and honest feedback culture encourages team members to share their opinions, ideas, and concerns. This helps identify issues early and fosters a collaborative and supportive work environment.

- **Documentation**: Proper documentation of decisions, processes, and changes ensures that everyone is on the same page. It also provides a reference point for future iterations and development stages.

- **Conflict Resolution**: Conflicts are inevitable in a collaborative environment. Having clear strategies for conflict resolution, such as mediation or consensus-building, helps keep the team focused and productive.

- **Stakeholder Management**: Keeping stakeholders informed and engaged throughout the development process is crucial. Regular updates, presentations, and reviews help manage expectations and secure buy-in.

3. Agile Development

Agile development is a popular methodology in product development, particularly in software. It emphasizes flexibility, collaboration, and rapid iteration. Agile teams work in short cycles, known as sprints, to deliver small, incremental improvements to the product.

Agile Practices

- **Scrum**: Scrum is a framework for managing and completing complex projects. It involves working in time-boxed sprints, with daily stand-ups, sprint reviews, and retrospectives. The Scrum team includes a Product Owner, Scrum Master, and Development Team.

- **Kanban**: Kanban is a visual system for managing work as it moves through a process. It helps teams visualize their workflow, limit work in progress, and optimize efficiency.

- **Continuous Integration/Continuous Deployment (CI/CD)**: CI/CD is a practice in which code changes are automatically tested and deployed to production. This approach enables rapid iteration and ensures the product is always in a deployable state.

- **User Stories**: User stories are short, simple descriptions of a feature or requirement from the user's perspective. They help the team focus on delivering value to the user and guide the development process.

Product development is a multifaceted process that involves ideation, prototyping, testing, and collaboration among cross-functional teams. By following a structured process and employing effective communication strategies, companies can develop innovative products that meet market needs and achieve business goals. From generating ideas through brainstorming to refining prototypes through iterative testing, each phase of product development plays a crucial role in bringing a successful product to market.

5. Planning and Strategy

Planning and strategy are essential for the success of product development, as they set the direction and long-term vision for the product and provide clear guidance for the development team and stakeholders. Effective planning includes creating a product roadmap, defining goals and KPIs, and prioritizing features. These elements are crucial to ensure that the product is developed in line with market expectations and business objectives.

Creating the Product Roadmap

The product roadmap is a strategic tool that provides an overall vision and a detailed plan for product development over time. It outlines the key milestones and stages that will guide the team through the various phases of the product lifecycle, from ideation to launch and beyond. A well-designed roadmap helps coordinate team activities, manage stakeholder expectations, and ensure that the product evolves according to market needs and business strategies.

1. Components of the Product Roadmap

Vision and Strategic Objectives: The roadmap begins with a clear definition of the product vision and long-term strategic objectives. This vision should align with the company's mission and overall goals and provide clear guidance on what the product should achieve and why it is important.

Milestones and Stages: The roadmap includes a series of key milestones and important stages in the product development process. These stages represent significant events, such as the completion of the prototyping phase, the launch of a beta version, and the official product release. Each milestone should have a target date and clearly defined success criteria.

Timelines and Deadlines: A crucial element of the roadmap is the planning of timelines. This includes estimating the time required to complete each phase of the project, from initial research and prototype development to testing and launch. Deadlines must be realistic, taking into account available resources and potential unforeseen circumstances.

Resources and Budget: The roadmap should consider the resources needed to complete each phase of the project. This includes human, technological, and financial resources. A detailed budget helps ensure that the project stays within the expected limits and that resources are allocated efficiently.

Risks and Mitigations: Identifying potential risks and developing mitigation strategies is essential for an effective roadmap. This allows the team to prepare for potential challenges and have contingency plans ready to address unforeseen issues and market changes.

2. Creating the Roadmap: Steps and Best Practices

Research and Analysis: The creation of the roadmap begins with an in-depth research and analysis phase. This includes analyzing market trends, customer needs, technical capabilities, and available resources. A clear understanding of these factors helps set realistic goals and plan project activities.

Stakeholder Involvement: It is important to involve all key stakeholders in creating the roadmap. This includes the development team, marketing, sales, customer support, and management. Their input is crucial to ensuring that the roadmap reflects the needs of all interested parties and that expectations are managed effectively.

Setting Priorities: Establishing priorities among various activities and milestones helps ensure that the team focuses on the most important aspects of the project. This can be done using methods such as the MoSCoW method (Must have, Should have, Could have, Won't have) to classify features and activities based on their importance.

Creating the Roadmap Document: Once all data has been gathered and priorities established, the roadmap document is created. This document should be clear, visually understandable, and easily updatable. Using visualization tools such as Gantt charts or project management software can help present the roadmap effectively.

Review and Update: The product roadmap is not a static document but must be reviewed and updated regularly. Any changes in market needs, available resources, or project requirements should be reflected in the roadmap to keep the project on track.

Setting Goals and KPIs

Goals and KPIs (Key Performance Indicators) are fundamental tools for measuring product success and guiding the team towards the desired outcomes. Goals define what the product should achieve, while KPIs provide specific metrics to monitor and evaluate progress toward these goals.

1. Setting Goals

SMART Goals: Goals should be SMART (Specific, Measurable, Achievable, Relevant, and Time-bound). This methodology ensures that goals are clear, realistic, and can be measured effectively.

- **Specific**: Goals should be clear and well-defined, answering questions like: What do we want to achieve? Why is it important? Who is involved?

- **Measurable**: It is essential to have concrete criteria for measuring success. This may include metrics like market share, number of users, or total sales.

- **Achievable**: Goals must be realistic and achievable with the available resources and time. They should be challenging but not impossible.

- **Relevant**: Goals should be pertinent and aligned with the overall business strategy. They should contribute to the company's success and have a significant impact.

- **Time-bound**: It is important to set clear deadlines for goals. This helps keep the team focused and ensures that progress is monitored regularly.

Examples of Goals:

- **Growth Goal**: "Increase the product's market share by 15% by the end of the year."

- **Customer Satisfaction Goal**: "Achieve a customer satisfaction score of 90% in feedback surveys within six months of launch."

- **Financial Performance Goal**: "Generate revenue of €1 million in the first quarter after the product launch."

2. Defining KPIs

Product Performance KPIs: KPIs measure product success based on established goals. Common KPIs include:

- **Number of Active Users**: Measures the number of users actively using the product regularly.

- **User Growth Rate**: Measures the percentage increase in the number of users over time.

- **User Engagement**: Measures how users interact with the product, such as time spent, features used, and usage frequency.

- **Conversion Rate**: Measures the percentage of users who complete a desired action, such as a purchase or sign-up.

- **User Retention**: Measures the percentage of users who continue to use the product after a specific period.

- **Feedback and Reviews**: Analyzes user feedback and reviews to evaluate satisfaction and identify areas for improvement.

Financial KPIs:

- **Revenue**: Measures the total revenue generated by the product.

- **Gross Profit**: Calculates gross profit by subtracting production costs from total revenue.

- **Customer Acquisition Cost (CAC)**: Measures the average cost to acquire a new customer.

- **Lifetime Value (LTV)**: Estimates the total value a customer brings during the entire product lifecycle.

3. Monitoring and Analyzing KPIs

Data Collection: Use analysis and reporting tools to collect data on KPIs. These tools can include data analytics software, dashboards, and reporting.

Results Analysis: Analyze the data collected to evaluate progress toward goals. Identify any deviations from targets and determine underlying causes.

Reports and Updates: Create regular reports to communicate results to team members and stakeholders. These reports should highlight successes, areas for improvement, and necessary corrective actions.

Adjustments and Optimizations: Based on KPI results, make adjustments to the strategy and project activities to improve goal achievement. This may include optimizing product features, modifying marketing strategies, or adjusting resources.

Feature Prioritization

Feature prioritization is a critical process to ensure that the developed product meets market needs and business objectives while optimizing the use of available resources. Prioritization helps decide which features to develop first, which can be postponed, and which might be excluded.

1. Prioritization Methods

MoSCoW Method: This method categorizes features into four categories:

- **Must Have**: Essential features that must be included in the final product.

- **Should Have**: Important but not critical features that can be included if time and resources allow.

- **Could Have**: Desirable but non-essential features that can be added if resources are available.

- **Won't Have**: Features that will not be included in the current product version but may be considered for future iterations.

Prioritization Matrix: Use a matrix to evaluate features based on criteria such as customer value, development cost, and business impact. The matrix helps visualize priorities and make informed decisions.

Value and Effort Assessment: Evaluate each feature based on the value it provides to the customer and the effort required to develop it. High-value, low-effort features should be prioritized.

Cost-Benefit Analysis: Compare the development costs of a feature with the expected benefits. This analysis helps decide whether the return on investment justifies the cost.

User and Stakeholder Feedback: Incorporate feedback from users and stakeholders into feature prioritization. User needs and expectations are key to determining the importance of different features.

2. Prioritization Process

Requirements Gathering: Start by gathering requirements from all stakeholders, including customers, sales teams, customer support, and marketing. Ensure all requirements are well-documented and understood.

Evaluation and Classification: Use prioritization methods to evaluate and classify features. This process may include prioritization workshops with the development team and stakeholders to discuss and agree on priorities.

Roadmap Development: Integrate

priority features into the product roadmap. This integration should consider timelines, resources, and dependencies between features.

Communication of Priorities: Clearly communicate priorities to the entire development team and stakeholders. Ensure everyone understands the reasons behind the decisions and how they will impact the project.

Monitoring and Review: Monitor progress in developing features and review priorities as necessary. Changes in the market, user feedback, or resources may require adjustments in prioritization.

Adaptations and Updates: Be ready to make adjustments to prioritization based on changes in requirements, resources, or market conditions. Flexibility is important to respond quickly to new opportunities or challenges.

Planning and strategy are fundamental pillars for the success of any product development project. Creating a product roadmap provides clear and structured guidance, while setting goals and KPIs ensures the project remains focused and measurable. Feature prioritization is crucial to ensuring that product development is efficient, effective, and aligned with market needs and business objectives. With proper planning and strategy, the development team can overcome challenges, meet expectations, and deliver a product that achieves lasting success.

6.Product Marketing

Product marketing is a crucial component for the success of any commercial offering. It encompasses the strategies and activities aimed at promoting and selling the product, enhancing its visibility, appeal, and relevance in the market. The main areas of product marketing include launch strategies, communication and branding, and marketing campaign management. An effective product marketing strategy can determine the product's success and its acceptance by the market.

Launch Strategies

The launch of a product is a critical moment in the product's lifecycle and can significantly influence its long-term success. A well-planned launch strategy must consider several aspects, including the target market, product positioning, and promotional tactics.

1. Launch Planning

Defining Objectives

First and foremost, it is essential to define the launch objectives. These objectives can vary depending on the nature of the product and the company's expectations. Some common objectives include:

- **Awareness Creation**: Generating interest and awareness of the product among the target audience.

- **Customer Acquisition**: Securing a defined number of customers or sales within the first weeks or months after launch.

- **Achieving Financial Milestones**: Reaching a certain revenue or profit volume within a specified period.

Market Analysis

An in-depth market analysis is fundamental for a successful launch. This analysis should include:

- **Market Segmentation**: Identifying the different market segments that might be interested in the product.

- **Competitor Analysis**: Studying competitors to understand how they position their products and which strategies they use.

- **Trend Research**: Identifying emerging trends that could influence the product's success.

Defining the Target

Identifying the target audience is crucial. This involves:

- **Customer Profiling**: Creating detailed profiles of ideal customers based on demographics, behavior, and preferences.

- **Customer Personas**: Developing

personas that represent the different segments of the target audience to direct communications and marketing strategies more effectively.

Development of the Launch Plan

The launch plan should detail activities and timelines. Key elements include:

- **Launch Timeline**: Establishing a clear schedule of pre-launch, launch, and post-launch activities.

- **Promotional Activities**: Planning promotional activities such as launch events, social media campaigns, and advertising.

- **Resource Management**: Allocating the necessary resources, including human, financial, and technical resources.

2. Launch Execution

Pre-Launch

During the pre-launch phase, it's important to generate excitement and prepare the market:

- **Teasers and Previews**: Using teasers and previews to spark interest and curiosity.

- **Influencer Engagement**: Collaborating with influencers and bloggers to increase visibility and obtain preliminary reviews.

- **Sales Channel Preparation**: Ensuring that all sales channels are ready and functioning.

Launch

Launch day must be carefully managed to ensure maximum impact:

- **Launch Event**: Organizing a launch event, whether physical or virtual, to present the product to the public.

- **Press Releases**: Distributing press releases to media and bloggers to gain media coverage.

- **Promotional Campaigns**: Launching targeted promotional campaigns across various channels, including social media, email marketing, and advertising.

Post-Launch

After the launch, it is crucial to continue supporting the product:

- **Performance Monitoring**: Monitoring sales, customer feedback, and other metrics to assess the launch's success.

- **Support and Assistance**: Providing customer support and assistance to resolve any issues and maintain high satisfaction.

- **Optimization**: Making adjustments to marketing and promotional strategies based on the results obtained and customer feedback.

Communication and Branding

Communication and branding are essential to creating an emotional connection with customers and differentiating the product from competitors. Strong branding helps establish a clear and consistent product image, while effective communication ensures the right message reaches the right audience.

1. Branding Development

Brand Identity

Brand identity consists of several elements that define how the product is perceived by the public:

- **Product Name**: Choosing a name that is

catchy, easy to remember, and relevant to the product.

- **Logo and Visual Design**: Creating a logo and visual design that represent the essence of the product and are easily recognizable.

- **Tone of Voice and Messaging**: Defining the tone of voice and messaging to be used in communications. This tone should reflect brand values and resonate with the target audience.

Value Proposition

The value proposition is a key element of branding. It should clarify:

- **Product Benefits**: What makes the product unique and why customers should choose it.

- **Differentiators**: The distinctive aspects of the product compared to competitors.

- **Problems Solved**: Which customer problems or needs the product addresses.

Creating the Brand Story

The brand story tells the story behind the product and the company. It should be engaging and authentic and may include:

- **Product Origins**: The story of how the product was created and what makes it special.
- **Mission and Vision**: The company's long-term goals and how the product contributes to achieving them.
- **Customer Experiences**: Stories and testimonials from satisfied customers.

2. Product Communication

Communication Strategies

Communication strategies must be designed to reach and influence the target audience:

- **Key Messages**: Defining the key messages that must be communicated in all marketing activities. These messages should be clear, consistent, and focused on the product's benefits.

- **Communication Channels**: Choosing the most suitable channels for communicating with the audience, including social media, email, online and offline advertising, and PR.

Content and Media

Creating content that captures attention and engages the audience:

- **Visual Content**: Using images, videos, and graphics to communicate messages effectively and attractively.

- **Blogs and Articles**: Publishing articles

and blogs that offer value to the audience and increase the product's visibility.

- **Testimonials and Reviews**: Sharing customer testimonials and reviews to build trust and credibility.

Reputation Management

Monitoring and managing the product's and brand's reputation:

- **Social Media Monitoring**: Following social media conversations to respond quickly to feedback and comments.

- **Crisis Management**: Having a crisis management plan to address any issues or controversies that may arise.

Marketing Campaign Management

Marketing campaigns are coordinated and planned strategies to promote a product or service. Effective marketing campaign management is essential to achieving sales and branding objectives.

1. Campaign Planning

Campaign Objectives

Defining the specific objectives of the campaign, which may include:

- **Increasing Awareness**: Making the product known to a wider audience.
- **Generating Leads**: Obtaining contacts from potential customers interested in the product.
- **Increasing Sales**: Boosting product sales within a specified period.

Targeting

Identifying the target audience for the campaign:

- **Segmentation**: Dividing the audience into segments based on characteristics such as demographics, behavior, and preferences.

- **Targeting**: Using data and analysis to direct campaigns toward the most relevant audience segments.

Budget and Resources

Establishing the budget and necessary resources for the campaign:

- **Budget Allocation**: Deciding how to allocate the budget among different channels and activities.

- **Human Resources**: Assigning teams and resources to manage and implement the campaign.

2. Campaign Execution

Content Creation

Developing content that attracts and engages the audience:

- **Messages and Offers**: Creating clear messages and special offers to incentivize action.
- **Design and Creativity**: Designing ads and marketing materials that are visually appealing and consistent with branding.

Channel Selection

Choosing the most appropriate marketing channels to reach the target audience:

- **Social Media**: Using platforms like

Facebook, Instagram, and LinkedIn for targeted campaigns.

- **Email Marketing**: Sending personalized emails to segmented contact lists.

- **Online Advertising**: Using Google Ads and other forms of online advertising to reach new customers.

Launch and Monitoring

Launching the campaign and monitoring its performance:

- **Implementation**: Executing the planned activities and launching the campaigns on the chosen channels.

- **Real-Time Monitoring**: Using analytics tools to monitor campaign performance in real-time and make adjustments if necessary.

3. Analysis and Optimization

Results Analysis

Evaluating the campaign's effectiveness through metrics and KPIs:

- **Performance Measurement**: Analyzing performance metrics such as clicks, impressions, conversions, and ROI.
- **Feedback and Results**: Collecting feedback from customers and analyzing results to determine what worked and what can be improved.

Optimization

Making changes and optimizing campaigns based on the results obtained:

- **A/B Testing**: Testing different versions of content and offers to determine which is more effective.
- **Strategy Adjustment**: Adapting

marketing strategies and reallocating the budget based on performance and observed trends.

Reports and Lessons Learned

Creating detailed reports on campaign performance and identifying lessons learned:

- **Final Reports**: Documenting the campaign's results, including successes and areas for improvement.

- **Lessons Learned**: Reflecting on the lessons learned and using this information to improve future campaigns.

Product marketing is a strategic function that requires careful planning and execution to ensure the product's success in the market. Launch strategies, communication and branding, and marketing campaign management are all crucial components of this process. A well-structured marketing strategy not only helps introduce the product to the market but also contributes to building a strong brand image and maintaining a continuous connection with the audience. The key to effective product marketing is the alignment between marketing strategies and business objectives, along with constant attention to market feedback and campaign results.

7. Monitoring and Feedback

Monitoring and feedback are essential components in product management and marketing strategy. These processes help ensure that the product meets user expectations, addresses market needs, and continuously improves over time. This document will explore in detail how to gather and analyze user feedback, measure product success through specific metrics, and implement an ongoing process of iteration and continuous improvement.

Gathering and Analyzing User Feedback

User feedback is a valuable resource that provides direct insights into how the product is perceived and used. Gathering and analyzing this feedback helps identify areas for improvement, resolve issues, and make strategic adjustments.

1. Methods for Collecting Feedback

Surveys and Questionnaires

- **Online Surveys**: Use tools like SurveyMonkey, Google Forms, or Typeform to collect feedback through online surveys. These tools can be designed to gather both quantitative and qualitative responses on various aspects of the product.

- **Post-Purchase Questionnaires**: Send questionnaires after purchase to obtain immediate feedback on the user experience. This may include questions about ease of use, satisfaction, and perceived value.

Interviews and Focus Groups

- **Direct Interviews**: Conduct personal or phone interviews with selected users to gain detailed and in-depth feedback. This method allows for a more detailed and personalized exploration of user opinions.

- **Focus Groups**: Organize focus groups with groups of users to discuss and collect feedback on specific aspects of the product. Focus groups provide diverse perspectives and facilitate in-depth discussions.

Review and Comment Analysis

- **Online Reviews**: Monitor reviews on platforms like Amazon, Yelp, and app stores. User reviews can provide insights into the product's strengths and weaknesses.

- **Social Media Comments**: Analyze comments and mentions on social media to gather spontaneous feedback and observe user discussions about the product.

Customer Support Monitoring

- **Support Tickets**: Examine support tickets and assistance requests to identify recurring issues and areas for improvement. Frequently asked questions and user-raised problems can provide valuable suggestions for optimizing the product.

- **Support Chats and Forums**: Analyze conversations in support chats and forums to gather feedback on user issues and needs.

2. Analyzing Feedback

Classifying Feedback

- **Positive Feedback**: Identify the product's strengths and aspects appreciated by users. This feedback can be used to emphasize strengths in marketing communications and branding strategies.

- **Negative Feedback**: Analyze criticisms and suggestions for improvement. It is important to classify issues based on their frequency and severity to address the most relevant issues first.

Identifying Recurring Themes

- **Qualitative Analysis**: Use qualitative analysis techniques, such as content analysis, to identify recurring themes and patterns in user feedback. This may include using text analysis software to extract common topics.

- **Clustering**: Group feedback into categories or clusters to identify common thematic areas. This helps focus improvement efforts on specific areas of the product.

Prioritizing Improvement Areas

- **Impact and Urgency**: Assess the impact and urgency of identified issues. Prioritize areas for improvement based on their relevance to the user experience and potential impact on product success.

- **Available Resources**: Consider available resources and the cost associated with implementing changes. Plan modifications based on their feasibility and expected benefits.

Success Metrics

Success metrics are essential tools for measuring the effectiveness of the product and marketing strategies. These metrics provide concrete data to evaluate whether the product is achieving its objectives and how it is performing relative to expectations.

1. Types of Metrics

Product Usage Metrics

- **Adoption Rate**: Measures the percentage of users who start using the product compared to the total number of potential users. A high adoption rate indicates good initial success of the product.

- **Usage Frequency**: Evaluates how often users engage with the product. Metrics like daily or monthly logins can indicate how integrated the product is into users' routines.

- **Usage Duration**: Measures the average duration of product use per session. Longer usage times may suggest that the product is engaging and satisfying.

Customer Satisfaction Metrics

- **Net Promoter Score (NPS)**: NPS measures the likelihood that a user would recommend the product to others. This score provides an indication of overall satisfaction and customer loyalty.

- **Customer Satisfaction Score (CSAT)**: CSAT measures customer satisfaction with a specific aspect of the product or service. It is generally collected through short surveys after key interactions or experiences.

Financial Performance Metrics

- **Revenue Growth**: Analyzes the growth of revenue generated by the product. Positive growth indicates that the product is generating value and attracting the market.

- **Customer Acquisition Cost (CAC)**:

Measures the average cost to acquire a new customer. A high CAC may indicate the need to optimize marketing strategies.

- **Lifetime Value (LTV)**: Estimates the total value a customer brings over the product's lifecycle. Comparing LTV with CAC helps evaluate the product's profitability.

Product Quality Metrics

- **Churn Rate**: Measures the percentage of users who stop using the product within a specific period. A high churn rate may indicate issues with customer satisfaction or product quality.

- **Problem Resolution Rate**: Evaluates the ability to resolve issues and support requests effectively. A high problem resolution rate indicates good customer service and effective problem management.

2. Monitoring Metrics Tools

Analytics Software

- **Google Analytics**: Use Google Analytics to monitor website traffic and user behavior. This tool offers a wide range of metrics to analyze product usage and interaction.

- **Data Analysis Tools**: Use tools like Tableau, Power BI, or Looker to visualize and analyze financial and operational metrics.

Dashboards and Reports

- **Custom Dashboards**: Create custom dashboards to monitor metrics in real-time. Dashboards should be set up to display the most relevant KPIs and provide immediate insights.

- **Periodic Reports**: Generate periodic reports to analyze product performance. These reports should include an analysis of metrics, results, and trends over time.

Iteration and Continuous Improvement

Iteration and continuous improvement are essential for maintaining product competitiveness and relevance. This process involves making modifications and improvements based on user feedback and success metrics.

1. Iteration Process

Data Collection and Analysis

- **Identifying Issues**: Use data and feedback to identify problems and areas for improvement. This may include resolving bugs, enhancing features, or adding new functionalities.

- **Defining Iteration Goals**: Set clear objectives for changes and improvements. Goals should be specific, measurable, and aligned with user needs and business strategies.

Development and Testing of Changes

- **Prototyping**: Create prototypes or beta versions of proposed changes to test new features or improvements. This allows for preliminary feedback and adjustments before official release.

- **Usability Testing**: Conduct usability tests to evaluate how users interact with changes and identify any usability issues.

Implementation and Monitoring

- **Gradual Release**: Implement changes gradually to minimize risks and monitor the impact on a limited user segment before a full release.

- **Post-Release Monitoring**: Monitor performance and feedback post-release to assess the effectiveness of changes and make any necessary adjustments.

2. Continuous Improvement

Feedback and Optimization Cycle

- **Iterative Cycle**: Adopt an iterative approach to continuous improvement, where changes are constantly tested and optimized based on user feedback and collected data.

- **Incorporating Feedback**: Ensure that user feedback is integrated into the development process and product roadmap to continually meet user needs.

Updates and Innovations

- **Regular Updates**: Plan regular product updates to address issues, introduce new features, and keep the product up-to-date with the latest trends and technologies.

- **Innovations**: Invest in research and development to explore new opportunities and innovations that can add value to the product and maintain market competitiveness.

Improvement Culture

- **Promoting a Culture of Improvement**: Create a company culture that values and encourages continuous improvement. This includes fostering an environment where team members are motivated to seek and implement improvements.

- **Training and Development**: Provide ongoing training and development for the product and marketing teams to ensure skills and knowledge are up-to-date and aligned with industry best practices.

Monitoring and feedback are fundamental processes for ensuring product success and continuous improvement. Collecting and analyzing user feedback provides valuable insights into how the product is perceived and used. Success metrics offer concrete data to evaluate product and marketing effectiveness. Iteration and continuous improvement ensure that the product remains relevant and competitive over time. Implementing a systematic process for monitoring, feedback collection, and continuous improvement is crucial for achieving and maintaining product success in the market.

8.Cross-Functional Collaboration

Product management is a complex process that requires intense collaboration across various business functions. The Product Manager (PM) must work closely with different teams to ensure that the product is developed, launched, and supported effectively. This section will explore in detail how the PM collaborates with sales and support teams, coordinates activities with the development team, and integrates marketing into the process.

Working with Sales and Support Teams

Collaboration with sales and support teams is crucial for the success of the product. These teams are often the first point of contact with customers and play a key role in gathering feedback and identifying opportunities for improvement.

1. Coordination with the Sales Team

Alignment of Goals

The PM must ensure that the sales team fully understands the product's value proposition and business objectives. This involves:

- **Training and Support**: Providing training on the product's strengths, key features, and positioning strategies. Sales representatives need to be well-informed about how the product compares to competing alternatives.

- **Sales Materials**: Creating and updating sales support materials, such as brochures, presentations, and case studies, to help the sales team effectively communicate the product's benefits.

Managing Customer Expectations

The PM should work with the sales team to:

- **Understand Customer Needs**: Gather and analyze information on customer needs and preferences. This data can help define product features and enhance the offering.

- **Update Product Roadmap**: Incorporate customer feedback and sales team requests into the product roadmap to ensure the product evolves in line with market needs.

Support During Launch

During the product launch, the PM must:

- **Launch Coordination**: Work with the sales team to plan and execute launch strategies, ensuring that the product is positioned correctly and marketing campaigns are synchronized with sales efforts.

- **Manage Feedback and Objections**: Assist the sales team in handling customer feedback and objections, providing timely responses and solutions.

2. Collaboration with the Support Team

Managing Support Requests

The support team is often the first to hear about user problems and requests. The PM must:

- **Training and Resources**: Provide the support team with the resources and information needed to resolve issues and answer customer questions. This can include detailed guides, FAQs, and technical training.

- **Monitor Issues**: Track support requests and recurring problems to identify areas for product improvement.

Gathering Feedback

The support team is a valuable source of user feedback. The PM should:

- **Collect Feedback**: Establish a system for collecting and analyzing user feedback provided by the support team.

- **Update the Product**: Use feedback to make improvements and address issues identified by users.

Proactive Support

The PM should:

- **Proactively Resolve Issues**: Work with the support team to proactively address issues and enhance the user experience.

- **Effective Communication**: Ensure clear and timely communication with the support team regarding product updates and feature changes.

Coordination with the Development Team

Coordination with the development team is essential to ensure that the product is built according to specifications and deadlines. This requires effective priority management and continuous communication.

1. Defining Requirements

Product Specifications

The PM must provide the development team with:

- **Requirements Documentation**: Create detailed documentation outlining product features, technical requirements, and quality expectations.

- **User Stories and Use Cases**: Develop user stories and use cases that describe how users will interact with the product.

Collaboration During the Development Cycle

Planning Meetings

- **Sprint Planning**: Participate in sprint planning meetings to ensure that priority features are included and deadlines are met.

- **Review Prototypes and Iterations**: Review prototypes and product iterations, providing feedback to ensure the final product meets expectations.

Managing Changes

- **Prioritizing Changes**: Work with the development team to manage changes and additional requests, ensuring that priorities are clear and resources are allocated effectively.

- **Communicating Changes**: Communicate changes and priority adjustments to the development team promptly and clearly.

2. Testing and Quality Control

Product Testing

- **Testing Plans**: Collaborate with the development team to create testing plans that ensure the product functions as intended and meets quality standards.

- **Feedback on Testing**: Provide feedback on test results and work together to address any issues identified during the testing phase.

Release and Monitoring

- **Release Planning**: Work with the development team to plan and manage the product release, ensuring that all issues are resolved and the product is ready for the market.

- **Post-Release Monitoring**: Monitor the product's performance post-release and collaborate with the development team to address any emerging issues.

Integration with Marketing

Marketing and product management must work closely to ensure that the product is positioned correctly and that marketing strategies align with the product's value proposition.

1. Marketing Planning and Strategy

Developing the Strategy

- **Roadmap Collaboration**: Work together to develop a marketing strategy that supports the product roadmap and its objectives.
- **Defining the Message**: Collaborate to

define key messages and value propositions to be used in marketing campaigns.

Marketing Materials

- **Content Creation**: Work with the marketing team to create promotional content, such as brochures, case studies, and website content.

- **Campaign Development**: Coordinate marketing campaigns with the marketing team to ensure that promotions and communications align with the product's features and benefits.

2. Product Launch

Launch Plan

- **Launch Strategy**: Collaborate with the marketing team to develop a detailed launch plan that includes events, press releases, and advertising campaigns.

- **Activity Alignment**: Ensure that marketing activities are well-coordinated with the product launch and that all resources are utilized effectively.

Monitoring and Optimization

- **Campaign Analysis**: Monitor marketing campaign performance and work with the marketing team to optimize strategies based on results.

- **Market Feedback**: Gather feedback from the market and customers and use this information to make improvements to marketing strategies.

Challenges in Product Management

The role of the Product Manager is complex and can face various challenges, including conflict management, navigating organizational changes, and adapting to new technologies.

1. Conflict Management

Internal Conflicts

- **Divergence of Opinion**: Conflicts may arise between the PM and other teams due to differing opinions on product priorities, features, and resources. It is essential to manage these conflicts through open communication and a common focus on business objectives.

- **Managing Expectations**: Balancing the expectations of different stakeholders, including the development team, marketing, and sales representatives, can be challenging. The PM must set clear priorities and communicate decisions transparently.

Customer Conflicts

- **Handling Criticism**: The PM must address customer criticisms and negative feedback constructively, using this information to make product improvements.

- **Effective Communication**: Managing customer expectations and resolving issues effectively is crucial to maintaining customer satisfaction and loyalty.

2. Navigating Organizational Change

Adapting to Changes

- **Corporate Restructuring**: Organizational restructuring can impact how the product is managed and launched. The PM must adapt to structural changes and new business priorities.

- **New Strategies and Objectives**: Changes in business strategy or objectives may require adjustments to the product roadmap. The PM needs to be flexible and adapt to new directions.

Communication and Alignment

- **Aligning with New Objectives**: Ensure that the product and marketing strategies are aligned with new business objectives and corporate strategies.

- **Change Management**: Communicate and manage change with the team and stakeholders to ensure everyone is aware of updates and new goals.

3. Adapting to New Technologies

Technological Evolution

- **Technology Updates**: Keeping up with new technologies and industry trends is essential to maintaining product competitiveness. The PM must stay informed about the latest technological innovations and assess their impact on the product.

- **Integrating New Technologies**: Integrating new technologies into the product can be complex and require significant changes in design and development. The PM must manage these integrations effectively.

Innovation and Experimentation

- **Promoting Innovation**: Encourage innovation within the team and explore new technological opportunities to enhance the product.

- **Testing New Technologies**: Evaluate and test new technologies to determine if they can be integrated into the product and add value.

Cross-functional collaboration is a critical aspect of product management, requiring alignment between sales, support, development, and marketing teams. Each team plays a significant role in the product's success, and the PM must ensure that all parties are aligned and working toward common goals. Managing challenges such as conflict, organizational changes, and technological advancements requires strong leadership and change management skills. Successfully addressing these challenges is essential for ensuring the product's success and continued growth.

Index

1. Introduction pg.4

2. The Product Life Cycle (Product Life Cycle) pg.25

3. Market Research pg.39

4. Product Development pg.59

5. Planning and Strategy pg.82

6. Product Marketing pg.97

7. Monitoring and Feedback pg.115

8. Cross-Functional Collaboration pg.128

www.ingramcontent.com/pod-product-compliance
Lightning Source LLC
Chambersburg PA
CBHW050257230526
45471CB00005B/1916